THE ENTHUSIAST

I'll Sleep When I'm Dead

Asa Eccleston Kibilski

CONTENTS

Title Page

Copyright

The Enthusiast Awakens: Unveiling the Ever-Curious Type Seven 1

Fueled by Fun: The Driving Force of the Enthusiast's Head Center 4

The Adventure Begins: Embracing the Enthusiast's Gut Instinct 8

Avoiding the Abyss: The Heart Center's Quest for Connection 12

Winged Wonders: Discovering Your 6 or 8 Influence 16

The Highs and Lows: Navigating the Emotional Rollercoaster 20

The Fear of Missing Out: Unmasking the Enthusiast's Core Anxiety 23

Scattered or Strategic?: Taming the Whirlwind of Thoughts 26

Always Planning the Next Thing: The Enthusiast's Relationship with Time 29

The Art of Reframing: Turning Negativity into Optimism 32

Cultivating Contentment: Finding Satisfaction in the Present Moment 36

Grounded in Gratitude: Practicing Appreciation for What Is 40

From FOMO to JOMO: The Joy of Missing Out 44

Embracing the Inner Critic: Transforming Self-Doubt into 48

Self-Compassion

Thriving as an Enthusiast: Creating a Life of Joyful Purpose   52

THE ENTHUSIAST AWAKENS: UNVEILING THE EVER-CURIOUS TYPE SEVEN

If you've ever been told you have boundless energy, a zest for life that's almost infectious, and an insatiable curiosity about the world, then chances are you're an Enneagram Type Seven, affectionately known as "The Enthusiast." But what does it truly mean to be a Seven, and how does this Enneagram type shape your thoughts, feelings, and actions?

This book is your invitation to embark on a journey of self-discovery, exploring the depths of your Enthusiast personality. We'll delve into the exhilarating highs and challenging lows, the driving forces behind your boundless optimism, and the shadows that can sometimes cloud your sunny disposition. Together, we'll uncover the secrets to harnessing your natural gifts, overcoming your core fears, and creating a life that's filled with joy, meaning, and a healthy dose of adventure.

Defining the Enthusiast

At their core, Enthusiasts are the quintessential optimists, always seeking out new experiences and opportunities for growth. They are driven by a deep desire for happiness and fulfillment, and they believe that the world is full of possibilities just waiting to be explored. Their infectious enthusiasm and playful nature can light up a room, and their quick wit and boundless energy make them captivating companions.

However, beneath this bubbly exterior lies a fear of being trapped or limited. Enthusiasts crave freedom and autonomy, and they will go to great lengths to avoid boredom or pain. This can sometimes lead them to become scattered, overextended, or even reckless in their pursuit of pleasure.

The Head, Heart, and Gut Triad

To understand the complexities of the Enthusiast, we need to explore the three centers of intelligence that shape our personalities: the head, heart, and gut. Each center plays a unique role in how we process information, make decisions, and interact with the world.

The Enthusiast, as a head type, is primarily driven by their thoughts and ideas. They are constantly analyzing, planning, and seeking out new information. This mental agility can be a great asset, but it can also lead to overthinking and a tendency to get lost in their heads.

While the head center is dominant for Sevens, they also have a strong connection to their gut center, which governs their instincts and intuition. This is what fuels their adventurous spirit and their willingness to take risks. However, it can also lead to impulsiveness and a lack of follow-through.

The heart center, which governs emotions and relationships, is the least developed for Enthusiasts. This doesn't mean they are incapable of deep connection, but they may struggle with vulnerability and emotional intimacy.

The Role of Wings

In addition to the three centers, each Enneagram type has two "wings" – the numbers on either side of their core type. For the Enthusiast, these are Six (The Loyalist) and Eight (The Challenger). Each wing adds a unique flavor to the core Seven personality, influencing their strengths, weaknesses, and overall worldview.

A Seven with a Six wing tends to be more cautious and detail-oriented, while a Seven with an Eight wing is often more assertive and ambitious. Understanding your wing can provide valuable insights into your specific tendencies and patterns of behavior.

Embarking on the Journey

As we embark on this journey together, we'll explore each of these aspects in greater detail. We'll delve into the Enthusiast's core motivations, fears, and desires. We'll examine the role of wings and how they influence our individual personalities. And most importantly, we'll provide practical tools and strategies for personal growth and transformation.

So, if you're ready to embrace your inner Enthusiast and discover the secrets to living a life of joy, passion, and purpose, turn the page and let the adventure begin!

FUELED BY FUN: THE DRIVING FORCE OF THE ENTHUSIAST'S HEAD CENTER

The Enthusiast, with their boundless energy and zest for life, is a prime example of a Head Center type within the Enneagram system. This means their primary way of processing the world is through their intellect and thoughts. Their minds are constantly buzzing with ideas, plans, and possibilities. They're naturally curious, always seeking new information and experiences to stimulate their minds and keep boredom at bay.

The Thinking Center's Strengths

As a Head Center type, Enthusiasts possess several strengths that stem from their active minds:

1. **Quick Wit and Intellectual Agility:** Sevens are known for their sharp minds and ability to think on their feet. They can quickly grasp new concepts, analyze situations from multiple angles, and come up with creative solutions to problems.

2. **Optimism and Positivity:** Their focus on the positive aspects of life fuels their natural optimism. They tend to see the glass as half full, even in challenging situations, and this hopeful outlook can be contagious to those around them.

3. **Enthusiasm and Passion:** Their passion for life is infectious. They approach new experiences with genuine excitement and eagerness, inspiring others to share in their joy and enthusiasm.

4. **Adaptability and Spontaneity:** Sevens are not afraid of change or uncertainty. In fact, they often thrive in unpredictable situations, using their quick thinking and adaptability to navigate new challenges and opportunities.

5. **Broad Interests and Open-Mindedness:** Their curiosity leads them to explore a wide range of interests and ideas. They are open-minded and receptive to different perspectives, always eager to learn and grow.

The Pitfalls of the Thinking Center

While the Head Center offers many advantages, it can also lead to certain challenges for the Enthusiast:

1. **Overthinking and Analysis Paralysis:** Their tendency to overanalyze situations can sometimes lead to indecision and inaction. They may get caught up in endless possibilities, struggling to commit to a single path or make a definitive choice.

2. **Difficulty Focusing and Staying Present:** Their minds are constantly racing, jumping from one thought to the next. This can make it difficult to stay focused on the present moment and fully engage in what's happening around them.

3. **Avoiding Difficult Emotions:** Sevens may use their intellect to avoid dealing with uncomfortable emotions or difficult situations. They may rationalize their way out of feeling pain or sadness, preferring to focus on the positive aspects of life.

4. **Scattered Energy and Lack of Follow-Through:** Their

enthusiasm for new ideas can sometimes lead to scattered energy and a lack of follow-through. They may start many projects but struggle to complete them, always chasing after the next exciting possibility.

5. **Intellectualizing Feelings:** Sevens may intellectualize their emotions rather than truly experiencing them. They may analyze their feelings instead of allowing themselves to feel them fully, leading to a disconnect between their head and heart.

Finding Balance and Integration

To thrive as an Enthusiast, it's crucial to find a balance between the strengths and challenges of the Head Center. This involves:

- **Cultivating Mindfulness:** Practicing mindfulness can help Sevens stay grounded in the present moment and fully experience their emotions, rather than intellectualizing them.
- **Setting Priorities and Focusing:** Learning to prioritize tasks and focus on one thing at a time can help Sevens overcome their tendency to get scattered and overwhelmed.
- **Embracing Difficult Emotions:** Allowing themselves to feel and process difficult emotions can help Sevens develop greater emotional intelligence and resilience.
- **Developing Follow-Through:** Setting realistic goals and breaking them down into smaller steps can help Sevens develop the discipline and perseverance to follow through on their commitments.
- **Connecting with the Heart and Gut:** Cultivating a deeper connection with their heart and gut centers can help Sevens integrate their emotions and instincts into their decision-making processes.

By understanding the dynamics of their Head Center and actively working to balance its strengths and weaknesses, Enthusiasts can unleash their full potential and live a life that's both joyful and fulfilling. This journey of self-discovery and growth is not always easy, but it is undoubtedly worth it. For when the Enthusiast learns to harness the power of their mind, they become an unstoppable force of creativity, inspiration, and joy.

THE ADVENTURE BEGINS: EMBRACING THE ENTHUSIAST'S GUT INSTINCT

While Sevens are known for their intellectual prowess, their adventurous spirit and zest for life are deeply rooted in their gut center. This instinctual center of intelligence governs our basic survival instincts, gut feelings, and deep-seated desires. For Enthusiasts, this center is a powerful driving force, propelling them towards new experiences, exciting challenges, and a life filled with spontaneity and joy.

The Gut Center's Influence on Enthusiasts

The gut center manifests in several key ways for Sevens:

1. **Craving for New Experiences:** Sevens have an insatiable appetite for novelty and excitement. They are drawn to new experiences like moths to a flame, always seeking the next adventure, the next thrill, the next opportunity to expand their horizons.

2. **Risk-Taking and Spontaneity:** Sevens are not afraid to take risks or step outside their comfort zones. They trust their gut instincts and embrace the unknown, often acting on impulse and making decisions on the fly.

3. **Action-Oriented and Energetic:** Their gut center fuels their boundless energy and drive. They are doers, not just dreamers, always looking for ways to turn their ideas into reality and make things happen.

4. **Optimism and Resilience:** Sevens have a natural

optimism that stems from their gut center's focus on survival and thriving. They believe that things will work out in the end, and this faith in the future helps them bounce back from setbacks and challenges.

5. **Decisiveness and Assertiveness:** Their gut instincts often guide their decision-making process. They trust their gut feelings and act on them decisively, often taking charge and leading the way.

The Pitfalls of the Gut Center

While the gut center can be a powerful asset for Enthusiasts, it can also lead to certain challenges:

1. **Impulsiveness and Lack of Forethought:** Their tendency to act on impulse can sometimes lead to impulsive decisions and actions that they later regret. They may not always consider the long-term consequences of their choices, focusing instead on the immediate gratification of their desires.

2. **Restlessness and Impatience:** Their constant need for stimulation and excitement can lead to restlessness and impatience. They may struggle to slow down, relax, and appreciate the present moment, always seeking the next adventure.

3. **Avoiding Pain and Discomfort:** Sevens may use their gut center's focus on pleasure and excitement to avoid dealing with difficult emotions or challenging situations. They may seek distractions or escape through external stimuli rather than facing their inner struggles.

4. **Difficulty with Commitment and Follow-Through:**

Their love of novelty and adventure can make it challenging for Sevens to commit to long-term goals or relationships. They may get bored easily or feel trapped by routine, making it difficult to stay the course and see things through to completion.

5. **Overstimulation and Burnout:** Their constant pursuit of excitement and stimulation can lead to overstimulation and burnout. They may push themselves too hard, neglecting their need for rest and relaxation, leading to exhaustion and a loss of vitality.

Embracing the Gut Center's Wisdom

To harness the full potential of their gut center, Enthusiasts can:

- **Cultivating Discernment:** Learning to distinguish between healthy gut instincts and impulsive urges can help Sevens make more informed decisions and avoid rash actions.
- **Practicing Patience and Mindfulness:** Developing patience and mindfulness can help Sevens slow down, appreciate the present moment, and find joy in simple pleasures.
- **Facing Challenges with Courage:** Embracing challenges as opportunities for growth can help Sevens develop greater resilience and inner strength.
- **Honoring Commitments:** Learning to honor their commitments, even when they feel restless or bored, can help Sevens cultivate deeper relationships and achieve long-term goals.
- **Balancing Activity and Rest:** Finding a healthy balance between activity and rest can help Sevens avoid burnout and maintain their energy and vitality.

By embracing the wisdom of their gut center and working to balance its strengths and weaknesses, Enthusiasts can live a life that's truly adventurous, fulfilling, and aligned with their deepest desires. Their gut instinct is a powerful compass that can guide them towards new experiences, exciting challenges, and a life filled with joy, spontaneity, and boundless possibilities.

AVOIDING THE ABYSS: THE HEART CENTER'S QUEST FOR CONNECTION

While Enthusiasts are known for their intellectual curiosity and adventurous spirit, their heart center—the emotional center of intelligence—plays a significant, albeit often less acknowledged, role in their lives. For Sevens, the heart center represents a paradox: a yearning for deep connection and intimacy, coupled with a fear of vulnerability and emotional pain. This chapter delves into the complexities of the Enthusiast's heart center, exploring their desire for connection, their strategies for avoiding emotional depth, and the path towards authentic intimacy.

The Heart Center's Influence on Enthusiasts

The heart center manifests in several ways for Sevens:

1. **Desire for Connection:** Beneath their extroverted and outgoing nature, Sevens have a deep yearning for connection and belonging. They want to be loved, accepted, and appreciated for who they are, flaws and all.

2. **Idealization of Relationships:** Sevens often idealize relationships and people, projecting their own positive qualities onto others. This can lead to unrealistic expectations and disappointment when others don't live up to their idealized image.

3. **Fear of Vulnerability:** Sevens may fear vulnerability and emotional intimacy, associating these with pain, loss, or rejection. They may avoid deep emotional connection, preferring to keep things light and fun.

4. **Focusing on the Positive:** Sevens tend to focus on the positive aspects of life and relationships, minimizing or ignoring negative emotions or conflicts. This can create a superficial sense of connection that lacks true depth and intimacy.

5. **Seeking Validation and Approval:** Sevens may seek validation and approval from others to feel good about themselves. They may prioritize external validation over internal self-worth, leading to a dependency on others for their sense of happiness.

The Pitfalls of the Heart Center

While the heart center can be a source of joy and connection for Enthusiasts, it can also lead to certain challenges:

1. **Avoiding Emotional Depth:** Their fear of vulnerability may lead Sevens to avoid deep emotional conversations or situations that require them to open up and share their true feelings.

2. **Superficial Relationships:** Their focus on fun and excitement may lead to superficial relationships that lack depth and intimacy. They may have many acquaintances but few close friends who truly know and understand them.

3. **Difficulty with Commitment:** Their fear of being tied down or limited may make it difficult for Sevens to commit to long-term relationships. They may fear losing their freedom or independence, leading to a pattern of serial dating or short-lived relationships.

4. **Emotional Repression:** Their tendency to focus on

the positive and avoid negative emotions can lead to emotional repression. They may suppress their sadness, anger, or fear, which can manifest in other ways, such as physical ailments or unhealthy coping mechanisms.

5. **Codependency:** Their need for validation and approval from others can lead to codependency. They may rely on others to make them feel good about themselves, sacrificing their own needs and desires in the process.

Cultivating Authentic Connection

To develop healthier relationships and deeper emotional intimacy, Enthusiasts can:

- **Embracing Vulnerability:** Learning to embrace vulnerability and share their true feelings can help Sevens build stronger and more authentic connections with others.
- **Practicing Emotional Awareness:** Developing greater emotional awareness can help Sevens identify and process their emotions in a healthy way, rather than suppressing or avoiding them.
- **Setting Boundaries:** Setting healthy boundaries can help Sevens protect themselves from emotional overwhelm and maintain their sense of self in relationships.
- **Developing Self-Compassion:** Cultivating self-compassion can help Sevens overcome their fear of vulnerability and embrace their imperfections, leading to greater self-acceptance and healthier relationships.
- **Seeking Support:** Seeking support from trusted friends, family, or a therapist can help Sevens navigate the challenges of the heart center and develop deeper emotional intimacy.

By exploring the complexities of their heart center, Enthusiasts can overcome their fears and insecurities, cultivate authentic connection, and experience the joy and fulfillment that comes from deep and meaningful relationships. This journey towards emotional intimacy is not always easy, but it is undoubtedly rewarding. For when Enthusiasts learn to open their hearts and embrace vulnerability, they discover a whole new dimension of love, joy, and connection that can enrich their lives in countless ways.

WINGED WONDERS: DISCOVERING YOUR 6 OR 8 INFLUENCE

While the core Enneagram Seven personality provides a solid foundation for understanding the Enthusiast, the influence of their neighboring wings adds nuanced layers to their character. The wings—Type Six (The Loyalist) and Type Eight (The Challenger)—each bring unique strengths, challenges, and perspectives to the Enthusiast's world. Understanding your dominant wing can provide valuable insights into your specific tendencies and patterns of behavior, ultimately leading to a deeper understanding of yourself and your path to growth.

Seven with a Six Wing (The Enthusiast-Loyalist)

Sevens with a Six wing tend to be more grounded and security-oriented than pure Sevens. While they share the Enthusiast's zest for life and love of adventure, they also crave stability and loyalty in their relationships and commitments. This wing combination often results in a unique blend of optimism and anxiety, enthusiasm and caution, spontaneity and planning.

Strengths:

- **Loyal and Committed:** They value deep connections and loyalty in relationships, often going above and beyond for those they care about.
- **Responsible and Reliable:** They take their commitments seriously and strive to be trustworthy and dependable.
- **Detail-Oriented and Practical:** Their Six wing brings a practical and detail-oriented approach to their enthusiastic pursuits, helping them plan and execute their ideas effectively.

- **Supportive and Encouraging:** They offer unwavering support and encouragement to others, often acting as cheerleaders and motivators.
- **Community-Oriented:** They value belonging to a group or community, finding comfort and security in shared experiences and connections.

Challenges:

- **Anxiety and Worry:** Their Six wing can amplify their anxieties and fears, leading to excessive worry and overthinking.
- **Self-Doubt and Insecurity:** They may struggle with self-doubt and insecurity, questioning their abilities and seeking reassurance from others.
- **Difficulty Making Decisions:** Their desire for security and fear of making the wrong choice can lead to indecision and analysis paralysis.
- **Overcommitting and Overextending:** Their loyalty and desire to please can lead them to overcommit and overextend themselves, taking on too much responsibility and neglecting their own needs.
- **Rebellion and Counterphobia:** In reaction to their anxiety, they may engage in rebellious or risky behavior to prove their independence and overcome their fears.

Seven with an Eight Wing (The Enthusiast-Challenger)

Sevens with an Eight wing tend to be more assertive, ambitious, and independent than pure Sevens. They share the Enthusiast's love of adventure and excitement, but they also possess a strong drive for power and control. This wing combination often results in a dynamic blend of enthusiasm and assertiveness, spontaneity and determination, optimism and resilience.

Strengths:

- **Confident and Assertive:** They possess a strong sense of self-assurance and are not afraid to speak their minds or take charge.

- **Ambitious and Driven:** They are motivated by a desire to achieve their goals and make a difference in the world.
- **Independent and Self-Reliant:** They value their independence and autonomy, preferring to rely on themselves rather than others.
- **Protective and Loyal:** They fiercely protect those they care about and are fiercely loyal to their friends and family.
- **Resilient and Resourceful:** They are able to bounce back from setbacks and challenges, using their resourcefulness and determination to overcome obstacles.

Challenges:

- **Domineering and Controlling:** Their desire for power and control can lead them to become domineering and overbearing, especially in relationships and group settings.
- **Impatience and Impulsiveness:** Their Eight wing can amplify their impulsiveness and impatience, leading to hasty decisions and rash actions.
- **Difficulty with Vulnerability:** They may struggle with vulnerability and emotional intimacy, viewing these as signs of weakness.
- **Conflict and Confrontation:** Their assertiveness and strong opinions can lead to conflict and confrontation with others.
- **Overstepping Boundaries:** Their desire for control may lead them to overstep boundaries and disregard the needs and feelings of others.

Identifying Your Dominant Wing

Determining your dominant wing is a personal journey of self-reflection and exploration. Consider which strengths and challenges resonate most with you, and how your wing influences your overall personality and behavior. There are many online resources and quizzes available that can help you identify your dominant wing, but ultimately, the most accurate assessment comes from deep introspection and honest self-awareness.

By understanding your dominant wing, you gain valuable insights into your unique strengths, challenges, and growth opportunities. This knowledge empowers you to make conscious choices, cultivate your strengths, and address your weaknesses, ultimately leading to a more fulfilling and authentic life as an Enthusiast.

THE HIGHS AND LOWS: NAVIGATING THE EMOTIONAL ROLLERCOASTER

One of the defining characteristics of the Enthusiast is their vibrant and dynamic emotional landscape. Their zest for life and boundless optimism can lead to exhilarating highs, but it can also make them susceptible to intense lows. This emotional rollercoaster is fueled by their core desire for happiness and their fear of pain, creating a complex and often contradictory emotional experience. This chapter explores the highs and lows of the Enthusiast's emotional world, shedding light on their emotional triggers, coping mechanisms, and strategies for finding balance and stability.

The Enthusiast's Emotional Highs

When Sevens are in their element, their emotional energy is contagious. They radiate joy, excitement, and a zest for life that draws others in. These emotional highs are characterized by:

- **Exuberance and Enthusiasm:** They experience a genuine excitement and passion for life, finding joy in simple pleasures and everyday experiences.
- **Optimism and Positivity:** Their natural optimism allows them to see the good in every situation, focusing on possibilities and potential rather than limitations.
- **Spontaneity and Playfulness:** They embrace spontaneity and playfulness, finding joy in the unexpected and delighting in new experiences.
- **Creativity and Inspiration:** Their boundless energy and enthusiasm fuel their creativity and inspire them to explore new ideas and possibilities.

- **Charisma and Charm:** Their infectious enthusiasm and positive energy make them charismatic and charming, attracting others to their vibrant personality.

The Enthusiast's Emotional Lows

While Sevens are known for their optimism, they are not immune to emotional lows. When their core fears are triggered or their expectations are not met, they can experience a range of negative emotions, including:

- **Anxiety and Restlessness:** Their fear of missing out can lead to anxiety and a constant feeling of restlessness, always seeking the next exciting experience to avoid boredom or pain.
- **Impatience and Frustration:** Their desire for immediate gratification and aversion to discomfort can lead to impatience and frustration when things don't go their way.
- **Disappointment and Disillusionment:** When their high expectations are not met, they can experience disappointment and disillusionment, leading to a sense of emptiness or dissatisfaction.
- **Avoidance and Escape:** They may try to avoid or escape from painful emotions through distractions, numbing activities, or substances, leading to a cycle of avoidance and emotional repression.
- **Self-Criticism and Shame:** When they feel they have failed or let others down, they can be harsh on themselves, experiencing self-criticism and shame.

Navigating the Emotional Rollercoaster

To navigate the emotional rollercoaster and find greater balance, Enthusiasts can:

- **Developing Emotional Awareness:** Becoming more aware of their emotions and triggers can help Sevens identify when they are starting to feel overwhelmed or stressed, allowing them to take steps to manage their emotions before they spiral out of control.

- **Practicing Self-Care:** Prioritizing self-care activities, such as exercise, meditation, and spending time in nature, can help Sevens regulate their emotions and reduce stress.
- **Seeking Support:** Talking to a trusted friend, family member, or therapist can provide a safe space for Sevens to process their emotions and develop healthy coping mechanisms.
- **Challenging Negative Thoughts:** Identifying and challenging negative thought patterns can help Sevens reframe their perspective and cultivate a more positive outlook.
- **Finding Healthy Outlets for Emotions:** Engaging in creative activities, physical exercise, or other healthy outlets can help Sevens express their emotions in a constructive way.

By understanding and navigating their emotional rollercoaster, Enthusiasts can harness the power of their emotions to fuel their creativity, passion, and joy. They can learn to embrace both the highs and lows, finding balance and stability in their emotional lives. With self-awareness, self-care, and support, Enthusiasts can create a life that is both exciting and fulfilling, full of joy, adventure, and meaningful connections.

THE FEAR OF MISSING OUT: UNMASKING THE ENTHUSIAST'S CORE ANXIETY

Beneath the Enthusiast's exuberant exterior lies a core anxiety that fuels their relentless pursuit of new experiences and constant craving for stimulation. This fear, often referred to as FOMO (Fear of Missing Out), is a driving force behind their behavior, shaping their choices, relationships, and overall approach to life. This chapter delves into the depths of the Enthusiast's FOMO, exploring its origins, manifestations, and the strategies for overcoming this underlying anxiety.

Understanding FOMO

FOMO is a complex emotion that stems from a deep-seated fear of being left out, missing out on opportunities, or not experiencing all that life has to offer. For Enthusiasts, this fear is particularly potent due to their natural optimism, curiosity, and desire for happiness. They believe that the world is full of exciting possibilities, and missing out on any of them can feel like a personal failure or a threat to their well-being.

The Manifestations of FOMO

FOMO can manifest in various ways for Enthusiasts:

1. **Constant Comparison:** They may constantly compare themselves to others, feeling inadequate or envious when they see others enjoying experiences or opportunities that they are not.

2. **Social Media Obsession:** They may spend excessive amounts of time on social media, scrolling through

feeds and comparing their lives to the curated highlights of others.

3. **Overcommitting and Overscheduling:** They may overcommit themselves to social events, activities, and obligations, fearing that saying no will lead to missing out on something important or fun.

4. **Difficulty Relaxing and Enjoying the Present Moment:** They may struggle to relax and enjoy the present moment, always anticipating the next exciting thing or worrying about what they might be missing out on.

5. **Impulsive Decision-Making:** They may make impulsive decisions based on the fear of missing out, without fully considering the consequences or long-term implications.

The Roots of FOMO

FOMO can stem from a variety of factors, including:

- **Childhood Experiences:** Early experiences of neglect, abandonment, or exclusion can create a deep-seated fear of being left out or forgotten.
- **Cultural Influences:** Our culture's emphasis on productivity, achievement, and social comparison can contribute to feelings of FOMO, creating a sense of pressure to constantly be doing, experiencing, and achieving more.
- **Personality Traits:** Certain personality traits, such as extroversion, neuroticism, and low self-esteem, can make individuals more susceptible to FOMO.

Overcoming FOMO

While FOMO can be a challenging emotion to overcome, there are several strategies that can help Enthusiasts manage and reduce their anxiety:

1. **Cultivating Mindfulness:** Practicing mindfulness can help Sevens stay grounded in the present moment, appreciating what they have rather than focusing on what they might be missing.
2. **Practicing Gratitude:** Taking time each day to reflect on the things they are grateful for can help Sevens shift their focus from lack to abundance.
3. **Setting Boundaries:** Learning to say no to commitments and activities that don't align with their values or priorities can help Sevens reduce their feelings of overwhelm and overcommitment.
4. **Limiting Social Media Use:** Reducing the amount of time spent on social media can help Sevens avoid the constant comparison and unrealistic expectations that can fuel FOMO.
5. **Focusing on Personal Values:** Identifying and prioritizing their personal values can help Sevens make decisions based on what truly matters to them, rather than fear of missing out.

By understanding and addressing the root causes of their FOMO, Enthusiasts can break free from the cycle of anxiety and comparison, and create a life that is rich, fulfilling, and aligned with their true desires. This journey of self-discovery and growth requires patience, self-compassion, and a willingness to face their fears head-on. But the rewards are immeasurable, as they open themselves up to the possibility of a life filled with joy, contentment, and genuine connection.

SCATTERED OR STRATEGIC?: TAMING THE WHIRLWIND OF THOUGHTS

Enthusiasts are renowned for their quick wit, intellectual curiosity, and the whirlwind of ideas that constantly swirl within their minds. This mental agility is a source of creativity, spontaneity, and adaptability, but it can also lead to a sense of overwhelm, distraction, and a lack of focus. This chapter explores the inner workings of the Enthusiast's mind, delving into their thought patterns, mental strategies, and the challenges and opportunities that arise from their active mental landscape.

The Enthusiast's Thought Patterns

The Enthusiast's mind is a vibrant and dynamic place, characterized by:

- **Rapid-Fire Thinking:** Their thoughts often move at lightning speed, jumping from one idea to the next in a rapid-fire fashion. This can make them quick learners and creative problem solvers, but it can also lead to a sense of overwhelm and difficulty focusing on a single task.

- **Future-Oriented Thinking:** They tend to focus on possibilities and potential, envisioning future scenarios and exciting opportunities. This can be a source of motivation and inspiration, but it can also lead to a neglect of the present moment and a difficulty appreciating what is already happening.

- **Optimistic Bias:** They have a natural optimism bias, which means they tend to focus on the positive aspects of situations and downplay or ignore potential negatives. This can be helpful in maintaining a positive outlook, but it can also lead to unrealistic expectations and a lack of preparedness for challenges.

- **Divergent Thinking:** They are skilled at divergent thinking, generating a wide range of ideas and possibilities. This can be a valuable asset in creative fields, but it can also lead to indecision and a difficulty choosing a single path to pursue.
- **Intellectualization:** They may intellectualize their emotions and experiences, analyzing and rationalizing their feelings rather than fully experiencing them. This can be a coping mechanism for dealing with difficult emotions, but it can also lead to a disconnect from their own inner world.

The Challenges of the Enthusiast's Mind

While the Enthusiast's active mind offers many advantages, it can also present certain challenges:

- **Distractibility and Lack of Focus:** Their racing thoughts and constant stream of ideas can make it difficult to focus on a single task or project, leading to procrastination and unfinished business.
- **Impulsiveness and Impatience:** Their desire for immediate gratification and aversion to boredom can lead to impulsive decision-making and a difficulty delaying gratification.
- **Anxiety and Overwhelm:** The sheer volume of thoughts and ideas can sometimes feel overwhelming, leading to anxiety and a sense of being scattered or unfocused.
- **Difficulty Prioritizing:** Their many interests and ideas can make it difficult to prioritize and choose which ones to focus on, leading to a feeling of being spread too thin.
- **Analysis Paralysis:** Their tendency to overthink and analyze can sometimes lead to a state of analysis paralysis, where they become so caught up in the details that they are unable to make a decision or take action.

Strategies for Taming the Whirlwind

Enthusiasts can learn to harness the power of their minds and overcome these challenges by:

- **Mindfulness and Meditation:** Practicing mindfulness and meditation can help Sevens slow down their racing thoughts, become more present in the moment, and develop a deeper awareness of their inner experience.
- **Setting Goals and Priorities:** Creating clear goals and priorities can help Sevens focus their energy and attention on what truly matters, avoiding the trap of chasing after every shiny new idea.
- **Time Management Techniques:** Implementing effective time management techniques, such as scheduling, task lists, and deadlines, can help Sevens stay organized and on track.
- **Learning to Say No:** Developing the ability to say no to commitments and opportunities that don't align with their goals or priorities can help Sevens avoid overcommitting and overextending themselves.
- **Embracing Stillness and Reflection:** Taking time for stillness and reflection can help Sevens process their thoughts and emotions, gain clarity, and make more intentional choices.

By developing self-awareness and implementing these strategies, Enthusiasts can tame the whirlwind of thoughts and harness their mental agility to create a life that is both fulfilling and productive. Their active minds are a powerful asset, capable of generating creative solutions, inspiring others, and bringing joy and enthusiasm to the world. With practice and intentionality, they can learn to channel their mental energy in a way that serves them and those around them, creating a life that is both exciting and meaningful.

ALWAYS PLANNING THE NEXT THING: THE ENTHUSIAST'S RELATIONSHIP WITH TIME

The Enthusiast's relationship with time is a fascinating paradox. They are often seen as living in the moment, embracing spontaneity, and seizing every opportunity for fun and adventure. However, beneath this carefree exterior lies a deep-seated preoccupation with the future and a relentless drive to plan and anticipate the next exciting thing. This chapter explores the complex relationship between Enthusiasts and time, examining their perception of past, present, and future, as well as their strategies for managing time and maximizing their experiences.

The Enthusiast's Time Orientation

Enthusiasts are primarily future-oriented, with their attention often focused on what's to come. They are drawn to the possibilities and potential of the future, always looking for new experiences and opportunities to fill their time. This future orientation manifests in several ways:

- Anticipation and Excitement: They experience a thrill of anticipation when looking forward to future events, activities, or experiences. This sense of excitement can fuel their motivation and drive, propelling them towards their goals.
- Planning and Scheduling: They often engage in extensive planning and scheduling, creating detailed itineraries and to-do lists to maximize their time and ensure they don't miss out on any opportunities.
- Restlessness and Impatience: Their focus on the future can sometimes lead to restlessness and impatience with

the present moment. They may struggle to slow down and appreciate what's happening now, always eager for the next thing.

- Avoidance of Painful Memories: They may avoid dwelling on painful memories or past mistakes, preferring to focus on the positive aspects of their past and the exciting possibilities of the future.

While the Enthusiast's future orientation can be a source of motivation and drive, it can also lead to challenges:

- Difficulty Staying Present: Their focus on the future can make it difficult to fully engage in the present moment, leading to a sense of detachment or disconnection from their current experiences.
- Overcommitment and Overscheduling: Their desire to maximize their time and experience everything can lead to overcommitment and overscheduling, leaving little time for rest, relaxation, or spontaneity.
- Anxiety and Stress: The constant anticipation of the future and fear of missing out can create anxiety and stress, leading to a feeling of overwhelm and a difficulty enjoying the present moment.
- Procrastination and Avoidance: Paradoxically, their focus on the future can sometimes lead to procrastination and avoidance of tasks or responsibilities that seem unpleasant or boring.

Strategies for Managing Time and Maximizing Experiences

Enthusiasts can develop a healthier relationship with time by:

- **Practicing Mindfulness:** Cultivating mindfulness can help Sevens become more present and aware of their thoughts, feelings, and sensations in the moment. This can help them slow down, appreciate their current experiences, and reduce their anxiety about the future.
- **Setting Realistic Goals and Priorities:** Creating clear

goals and priorities can help Sevens focus their energy and attention on what truly matters, avoiding the trap of overcommitting and overextending themselves.

- **Scheduling Downtime and Relaxation:** Intentionally scheduling downtime and relaxation into their schedules can help Sevens avoid burnout and ensure they have time to recharge and replenish their energy.
- **Learning to Delegate and Say No:** Delegating tasks and learning to say no to commitments that don't align with their priorities can help Sevens free up time and energy for the things that truly matter.
- **Embracing Spontaneity:** While planning is important, allowing for spontaneity and flexibility can help Sevens embrace the unexpected and enjoy the present moment more fully.

By developing a more balanced and mindful approach to time, Enthusiasts can harness the power of their future orientation to create a life that is both exciting and fulfilling. They can learn to embrace the present moment while still planning for the future, creating a harmonious balance between spontaneity and intentionality. With practice and awareness, they can cultivate a relationship with time that allows them to fully experience and enjoy all that life has to offer, without sacrificing their well-being or happiness.

THE ART OF REFRAMING: TURNING NEGATIVITY INTO OPTIMISM

Enthusiasts are renowned for their optimistic outlook and ability to find the silver lining in even the most challenging situations. This natural inclination towards positivity is a valuable asset, allowing them to maintain hope, resilience, and a zest for life even in the face of adversity. However, this tendency can also be a double-edged sword, potentially leading to avoidance of difficult emotions, denial of reality, or a superficial approach to life's challenges. This chapter explores the art of reframing, a powerful tool that Enthusiasts can use to harness their natural optimism while still acknowledging and addressing negative experiences.

The Power of Reframing

Reframing is a cognitive technique that involves shifting your perspective on a situation, event, or thought. By changing the way you interpret or frame an experience, you can change your emotional response to it. For Enthusiasts, reframing can be a powerful tool for managing difficult emotions, maintaining optimism, and finding opportunities for growth and learning in challenging situations.

The Enthusiast's Reframing Strategies

Enthusiasts often employ several reframing strategies to maintain their positive outlook:

1. Focusing on the Positive: They naturally gravitate towards the positive aspects of a situation, emphasizing the good and downplaying the bad. This can help them maintain hope and motivation even in difficult times.

2. Seeking Opportunities: They look for opportunities for growth and learning in every experience, even those that are initially perceived as negative. This allows them to reframe challenges as stepping stones towards personal development.

3. Humor and Lightheartedness: They use humor and lightheartedness to diffuse tension and defuse negative emotions. This can help them maintain a positive attitude and avoid getting bogged down in negativity.

4. Future-Oriented Thinking: They focus on the future possibilities and potential outcomes of a situation, rather than dwelling on the negative aspects of the present. This can help them maintain hope and motivation for the future.

5. Reinterpreting Meaning: They may reinterpret the meaning of a negative experience, finding a silver lining or a lesson learned. This can help them make sense of difficult situations and find meaning in their struggles.

The Risks of Reframing

While reframing can be a valuable tool, it's important for Enthusiasts to be aware of its potential pitfalls:

- Toxic Positivity: Overusing reframing can lead to toxic positivity, where negative emotions are invalidated or dismissed. This can prevent individuals from processing their emotions in a healthy way and may lead to emotional repression.

- Denial of Reality: Reframing can sometimes become a form of denial, where individuals refuse to acknowledge the negative aspects of a situation or their own role in it. This can prevent them from taking responsibility for their actions or learning from their mistakes.

- Superficiality: Excessive reliance on reframing can lead to a superficial approach to life, where individuals gloss over problems or avoid dealing with difficult emotions. This can prevent them from experiencing true intimacy and connection with others.

Finding Balance and Authenticity

To use reframing effectively, Enthusiasts can:

- Acknowledging the Full Spectrum of Emotions: It's important to acknowledge and validate all emotions, both positive and negative. Reframing doesn't mean denying the existence of negative emotions, but rather finding a way to process them in a healthy and productive way.
- Practicing Self-Compassion: Being kind and understanding towards oneself during difficult times can help Enthusiasts avoid self-blame and shame, allowing them to learn and grow from their experiences.
- Seeking Support: Talking to a trusted friend, family member, or therapist can provide a safe space for Enthusiasts to process their emotions and develop healthy coping mechanisms.
- Balancing Optimism with Realism: While optimism is a valuable asset, it's important to balance it with realism and a willingness to face challenges head-on. This allows for a more nuanced and authentic approach to life.
- Embracing Vulnerability: Allowing oneself to be vulnerable and open to the full range of human emotions can lead to deeper connections with others and a more meaningful life experience.

By mastering the art of reframing, Enthusiasts can harness the power of their natural optimism while still acknowledging and addressing the challenges and complexities of life. This balanced approach allows them to maintain their positive outlook while still remaining grounded in reality, fostering resilience, growth, and authentic connection with themselves and others.

CULTIVATING CONTENTMENT: FINDING SATISFACTION IN THE PRESENT MOMENT

One of the most profound paradoxes for the Enthusiast is their relentless pursuit of future happiness, often at the expense of fully experiencing and appreciating the present moment. While their optimism and eagerness for new experiences are admirable traits, the constant focus on what's next can lead to a sense of dissatisfaction and a fleeting sense of joy. This chapter delves into the concept of contentment, exploring how Enthusiasts can cultivate a deeper sense of satisfaction and fulfillment in the here and now, without sacrificing their zest for life or their dreams for the future.

Understanding Contentment

Contentment is not about complacency or settling for less than you deserve. It is a state of inner peace and satisfaction that arises from appreciating and accepting what is present in your life, without constantly yearning for something more or different. For Enthusiasts, cultivating contentment can be a transformative experience, allowing them to fully savor their joys, navigate their challenges with grace, and create a life that is both exciting and fulfilling.

The Enthusiast's Challenges with Contentment

Enthusiasts may struggle with contentment due to several factors:

- Fear of Missing Out (FOMO): Their fear of missing out can lead them to constantly seek new experiences and opportunities, leaving little time or energy to appreciate what they already have.

- Hedonic Adaptation: They may experience hedonic adaptation, a phenomenon where the initial thrill of a new experience quickly fades, leaving them wanting more and constantly chasing after the next high.
- Comparison and Envy: Their tendency to compare themselves to others can lead to feelings of envy and dissatisfaction, making it difficult to appreciate their own unique blessings and accomplishments.
- Restlessness and Impatience: Their desire for immediate gratification and aversion to boredom can make it challenging to slow down, relax, and simply be present in the moment.

Cultivating Contentment

Enthusiasts can cultivate contentment by:

1. Practicing Gratitude: Taking time each day to reflect on the things they are grateful for can help Enthusiasts shift their focus from lack to abundance, fostering a sense of appreciation and contentment.

2. Savoring Positive Experiences: Intentionally savoring positive experiences, whether it's a delicious meal, a beautiful sunset, or a meaningful conversation, can help Enthusiasts prolong the joy and satisfaction they derive from these experiences.

3. Mindfulness and Presence: Practicing mindfulness and presence can help Enthusiasts become more aware of the present moment, allowing them to fully experience and appreciate the simple joys and pleasures of life.

4. Setting Realistic Expectations: Recognizing that no experience or achievement will bring lasting happiness can help Enthusiasts avoid the trap of constantly chasing after the next big thing.

5. Finding Joy in the Journey: Shifting their focus from achieving goals to enjoying the process of pursuing them can help Enthusiasts find more meaning and satisfaction in their daily lives.

6. Cultivating Self-Compassion: Practicing self-compassion can help Enthusiasts accept their imperfections and shortcomings, reducing the pressure to constantly strive for more and be better.

7. Embracing Simplicity: Simplifying their lives by decluttering, reducing commitments, and prioritizing what truly matters can help Enthusiasts create more space for peace, joy, and contentment.

The Benefits of Contentment

Cultivating contentment can bring numerous benefits to the Enthusiast's life:

- Reduced Anxiety and Stress: By focusing on the present moment and appreciating what they have, Enthusiasts can reduce their anxiety and stress levels.
- Increased Happiness and Well-being: Contentment is closely linked to happiness and overall well-being, as it allows individuals to experience more joy and satisfaction in their daily lives.
- Stronger Relationships: When Enthusiasts are content with themselves and their lives, they are more likely to cultivate deeper and more meaningful connections with others.
- Greater Resilience: Contentment can foster resilience, helping Enthusiasts bounce back from setbacks and challenges with greater ease and optimism.
- Enhanced Creativity and Productivity: When they are not constantly distracted by the pursuit of more, Enthusiasts can

channel their energy and focus into creative endeavors and productive pursuits.

By cultivating contentment, Enthusiasts can transform their relationship with themselves, their experiences, and the world around them. They can learn to appreciate the simple joys of life, find satisfaction in the present moment, and create a life that is both exciting and fulfilling. This journey towards contentment is not about giving up on their dreams or aspirations, but rather about finding a balance between pursuing their goals and appreciating the journey along the way.

GROUNDED IN GRATITUDE: PRACTICING APPRECIATION FOR WHAT IS

The Enthusiast's natural inclination towards optimism and future-oriented thinking can sometimes overshadow their ability to fully appreciate the present moment and the blessings they already have. While their enthusiasm and zest for life are admirable qualities, cultivating a deeper sense of gratitude can ground them in the present, enhance their well-being, and deepen their connection to themselves and the world around them. This chapter explores the transformative power of gratitude for Enthusiasts, offering practical strategies for cultivating a grateful heart and reaping the numerous benefits of this powerful emotion.

Understanding Gratitude

Gratitude is more than just saying "thank you." It is a deep appreciation for the goodness in our lives, a recognition of the positive aspects of our experiences, relationships, and circumstances. For Enthusiasts, gratitude can serve as a powerful antidote to their FOMO, anxiety, and restlessness, anchoring them in the present moment and fostering a sense of contentment and well-being.

The Benefits of Gratitude for Enthusiasts

Practicing gratitude can offer numerous benefits for Enthusiasts:

1. Reduced Stress and Anxiety: Focusing on what they are grateful for can help Sevens shift their attention away from their worries and fears, reducing stress and anxiety.

2. Increased Happiness and Well-being: Gratitude has been linked to increased happiness, life satisfaction, and overall well-being. It can help Sevens cultivate a more positive outlook and experience greater joy in their daily lives.

3. Improved Relationships: Expressing gratitude towards others can strengthen relationships, foster intimacy, and increase feelings of connection and belonging.

4. Enhanced Resilience: Gratitude can help Sevens develop greater resilience in the face of challenges and setbacks, allowing them to bounce back from adversity with greater ease and optimism.

5. Increased Self-Esteem: Recognizing and appreciating their own strengths and accomplishments can boost self-esteem and self-worth, reducing their reliance on external validation.

Cultivating Gratitude

There are many ways for Enthusiasts to cultivate gratitude in their daily lives:

1. Gratitude Journaling: Taking a few minutes each day to write down things they are grateful for can help Sevens focus on the positive aspects of their lives and cultivate a more grateful mindset.

2. Gratitude Meditation: Engaging in gratitude meditation, where they focus on feelings of appreciation and thankfulness, can help Sevens cultivate a deeper sense of gratitude and inner peace.

3. Gratitude Letters and Notes: Writing letters or notes expressing gratitude to friends, family members, or mentors can help Sevens strengthen their relationships and express their appreciation for the people in their lives.

4. Gratitude Rituals: Creating simple gratitude rituals, such as saying grace before meals or expressing gratitude at the end of each day, can help Sevens integrate gratitude into their daily routines.

5. Gratitude Walks: Taking walks in nature and focusing on the beauty and wonder of the natural world can help Sevens cultivate a sense of awe and appreciation for the world around them.

Integrating Gratitude into Daily Life

Enthusiasts can integrate gratitude into their daily lives by:

- Expressing Gratitude for Everyday Experiences: Notice and appreciate the small things in life, such as a delicious cup of coffee, a beautiful sunset, or a kind gesture from a stranger.
- Celebrating Achievements and Milestones: Take time to acknowledge and celebrate their own accomplishments, as well as the achievements of others.
- Finding Gratitude in Challenges: Look for the lessons and growth opportunities in challenging situations, rather than dwelling on the negative aspects.
- Sharing Gratitude with Others: Expressing gratitude to others, whether through words, actions, or gifts, can strengthen relationships and create a ripple effect of positivity.
- Making Gratitude a Habit: By practicing gratitude regularly, Enthusiasts can create a habit of appreciation and cultivate a more positive and fulfilling life experience.

By embracing gratitude, Enthusiasts can transform their relationship with themselves, their experiences, and the world around them. They can learn to appreciate the present moment, find joy in simple pleasures, and cultivate a deeper sense of connection and belonging. Gratitude is a powerful tool that can help Enthusiasts overcome their fear of missing out, anxiety, and restlessness, allowing them to live a life that is rich, meaningful, and full of gratitude.

FROM FOMO TO JOMO: THE JOY OF MISSING OUT

Enthusiasts, with their insatiable curiosity and zest for life, are often plagued by the Fear of Missing Out (FOMO). This pervasive anxiety can drive them to overcommit, overschedule, and constantly seek out new experiences, leaving them feeling exhausted and unfulfilled. However, there is an alternative to this relentless pursuit of more: JOMO, the Joy of Missing Out. This chapter explores the concept of JOMO, offering Enthusiasts a refreshing perspective on rest, relaxation, and the profound joy that can be found in simply being.

Understanding JOMO

JOMO is the antithesis of FOMO. It is a conscious choice to embrace stillness, solitude, and the simple pleasures of life, without feeling the need to constantly chase after the next big thing. For Enthusiasts, JOMO can be a transformative practice, allowing them to recharge their batteries, connect with their inner selves, and cultivate a deeper sense of contentment and well-being.

The Benefits of JOMO for Enthusiasts

Embracing JOMO can offer numerous benefits for Enthusiasts:

1. Reduced Stress and Anxiety: Stepping back from the constant pursuit of more can help Sevens reduce their stress and anxiety levels, allowing them to relax and recharge.

2. Increased Creativity and Productivity: By allowing their minds to rest and wander, Enthusiasts can tap into their creativity and find new inspiration for their projects and pursuits.

3. Deeper Self-Awareness: Spending time in solitude and reflection can help Sevens connect with their inner selves, gain clarity on their values and priorities, and make more intentional choices about how they spend their time and energy.

4. Improved Relationships: By prioritizing rest and relaxation, Enthusiasts can show up more fully in their relationships, offering their loved ones their undivided attention and presence.

5. Enhanced Well-being: JOMO can lead to a greater sense of overall well-being, as it allows Enthusiasts to prioritize their physical, emotional, and mental health.

Cultivating JOMO

Enthusiasts can cultivate JOMO by:

1. Scheduling Downtime: Intentionally scheduling downtime into their calendars can help Sevens prioritize rest and relaxation, ensuring they have time to recharge and rejuvenate.

2. Unplugging from Technology: Taking breaks from social media, email, and other digital distractions can help Sevens disconnect from the constant stream of information and focus on the present moment.

3. Engaging in Restorative Activities: Engaging in activities that promote relaxation and restoration, such as meditation, yoga, reading, spending time in nature, or simply doing nothing, can help Sevens recharge their batteries and reduce stress.

4. Saying No to Commitments: Learning to say no to social invitations, work projects, or other commitments that don't align with their priorities can help Sevens create more space for JOMO in their lives.

5. Embracing Solitude: Spending time alone can be a valuable opportunity for self-reflection, creativity, and personal growth. Enthusiasts can embrace solitude by journaling, meditating, taking walks in nature, or simply enjoying their own company.

6. Redefining Productivity: Shifting their definition of productivity from constantly doing to simply being can help Enthusiasts release the pressure to always be on the go and appreciate the value of rest and relaxation.

Integrating JOMO into Daily Life

Enthusiasts can integrate JOMO into their daily lives by:

- Creating Rituals for Rest and Relaxation: Establish regular routines for rest and relaxation, such as taking a warm bath before bed, reading a book in the afternoon, or enjoying a quiet cup of tea in the morning.
- Setting Boundaries with Technology: Set limits on screen time and create tech-free zones in their homes or workplaces to encourage more offline activities and interactions.
- Prioritizing Self-Care: Make time for activities that nourish their physical, emotional, and mental well-being, such as exercise, healthy eating, sleep, and creative expression.
- Embracing the Power of Saying No: Practice saying no to invitations or requests that don't align with their priorities or that would leave them feeling overwhelmed or drained.
- Celebrating Moments of Stillness: Find joy in the simple moments of stillness and silence, whether it's watching the clouds drift by, listening to the birds sing, or simply enjoying

the peace of their own company.

By embracing JOMO, Enthusiasts can transform their relationship with time, productivity, and well-being. They can learn to appreciate the value of rest and relaxation, cultivate a deeper connection with themselves, and create a life that is both exciting and fulfilling. JOMO is not about giving up on their dreams or ambitions, but rather about finding a healthier balance between pursuing their goals and nurturing their inner selves. It is about recognizing that true joy and fulfillment often come from slowing down, savoring the present moment, and simply being.

EMBRACING THE INNER CRITIC: TRANSFORMING SELF-DOUBT INTO SELF-COMPASSION

Enthusiasts, with their boundless energy and optimistic outlook, may appear immune to self-doubt. However, beneath their cheerful exterior, many Sevens grapple with an inner critic that whispers doubts and insecurities. This critical voice can undermine their confidence, fuel their fear of missing out, and lead to a constant striving for external validation. This chapter explores the origins and manifestations of the Enthusiast's inner critic, offering strategies for embracing self-compassion and transforming self-doubt into a catalyst for growth.

Understanding the Inner Critic

The inner critic is an internalized voice that judges, criticizes, and doubts our abilities, worth, and lovability. For Enthusiasts, this voice may manifest as a fear of not being good enough, interesting enough, or successful enough. It can also fuel their fear of missing out, as they strive to prove their worth through constant activity and achievement.

The Inner Critic's Manifestations

The inner critic can manifest in various ways for Enthusiasts:

1. **Negative Self-Talk:** They may engage in negative self-talk, putting themselves down, focusing on their flaws, and doubting their abilities.

2. **Comparison and Competition:** They may compare themselves to others, feeling inferior or inadequate when they perceive others as more successful,

attractive, or accomplished.

3. **Perfectionism:** They may strive for perfection in all areas of their lives, fearing that anything less than perfect is not good enough.

4. **Fear of Failure:** They may fear failure and avoid taking risks, believing that any misstep will confirm their inadequacy.

5. **People-Pleasing:** They may try to please everyone, fearing that disapproval or rejection will confirm their unworthiness.

The Origins of the Inner Critic

The inner critic often develops in childhood, as a result of negative experiences, criticism, or conditional love. For Enthusiasts, this voice may be amplified by their fear of pain and discomfort, as well as their desire for external validation.

Embracing Self-Compassion

Self-compassion is a powerful antidote to the inner critic. It involves treating oneself with kindness, understanding, and acceptance, even in the face of mistakes, failures, or shortcomings. For Enthusiasts, cultivating self-compassion can be a transformative experience, allowing them to silence their inner critic and embrace their whole selves, flaws and all.

Strategies for Cultivating Self-Compassion

Enthusiasts can cultivate self-compassion by:

1. **Recognizing the Inner Critic:** The first step is to become aware of the inner critic's voice and its negative impact on their thoughts and feelings.
2. **Challenging Negative Self-Talk:** When the inner critic

speaks, challenge its negative messages with positive affirmations and self-affirming statements.

3. **Practicing Self-Kindness:** Treat themselves with kindness and understanding, as they would a good friend. Offer themselves words of encouragement and support, especially during difficult times.
4. **Focusing on Strengths:** Focus on their strengths and accomplishments, rather than dwelling on their flaws and shortcomings. Celebrate their successes and acknowledge their unique gifts and talents.
5. **Mindful Self-Reflection:** Engage in mindful self-reflection, observing their thoughts and feelings without judgment. This can help them develop a more compassionate and accepting relationship with themselves.
6. **Forgiveness and Acceptance:** Forgive themselves for their mistakes and imperfections, recognizing that everyone makes mistakes and that these experiences are opportunities for growth and learning.
7. **Seeking Support:** Seek support from trusted friends, family members, or a therapist who can offer a listening ear, validation, and encouragement.

Transforming Self-Doubt into Self-Compassion

By embracing self-compassion, Enthusiasts can transform their relationship with themselves and their inner critic. They can learn to quiet the negative voice of self-doubt and replace it with a kinder, more accepting inner dialogue. This shift can lead to increased self-esteem, greater resilience, and a more fulfilling life experience.

As Enthusiasts learn to embrace their imperfections and accept themselves as they are, they free themselves from the constant need for external validation. They can pursue their goals and dreams with confidence, knowing that their worth is not dependent on their achievements or the approval of others. By cultivating self-compassion, Enthusiasts can unleash their full potential and live a life that is authentic, joyful, and aligned with their true values and desires.

THRIVING AS AN ENTHUSIAST: CREATING A LIFE OF JOYFUL PURPOSE

We've embarked on a thrilling journey through the vibrant landscape of the Enthusiast, exploring their strengths, challenges, and the intricate dance between their head, heart, and gut centers. We've delved into their fear of missing out, their quest for contentment, and their boundless optimism. Now, as we approach the final chapter, it's time to synthesize these insights and discover how Enthusiasts can truly thrive, creating a life that is both joyful and purposeful.

Embracing Your Enthusiasm

The Enthusiast's greatest gift is their infectious enthusiasm for life. It's the spark that ignites their passions, fuels their creativity, and draws others into their orbit. Embracing this enthusiasm means:

- **Celebrating Your Strengths:** Recognize and celebrate your natural gifts of optimism, curiosity, and zest for life. These are the qualities that make you unique and bring joy to the world.
- **Following Your Passions:** Identify and pursue your passions with gusto. Don't be afraid to try new things, explore different interests, and discover what truly lights you up.
- **Sharing Your Joy:** Share your enthusiasm with others. Your positive energy can be contagious, inspiring and uplifting those around you.

Navigating Your Challenges

While enthusiasm is a powerful force, it's important to be mindful of the challenges that can arise from this personality type. These challenges include:

- **Overcoming FOMO:** Develop strategies for managing your fear of missing out, such as practicing mindfulness, gratitude, and setting boundaries.
- **Cultivating Contentment:** Learn to appreciate the present moment and find satisfaction in what you already have, rather than constantly chasing after the next big thing.
- **Balancing Spontaneity with Responsibility:** While spontaneity can be fun, it's important to balance it with responsibility and commitment. Learn to follow through on your commitments and honor your obligations to others.
- **Embracing Vulnerability:** Allow yourself to be vulnerable and express your true feelings, even if it means risking rejection or disappointment. Authentic connection is essential for a fulfilling life.

Finding Your Purpose

As an Enthusiast, your purpose lies in using your natural gifts to bring joy, inspiration, and positive change to the world. This could manifest in a variety of ways, depending on your individual passions and interests. Perhaps you're meant to be a creative innovator, a passionate advocate for a cause you believe in, or a joyful educator who inspires others to learn and grow.

Your purpose may also involve helping others overcome their own fears and anxieties, guiding them towards a more optimistic and fulfilling life. As you learn to navigate your own challenges and embrace your full potential, you become a beacon of hope and possibility for others.

Creating a Life of Joyful Purpose

To create a life of joyful purpose, consider the following steps:

1. **Self-Reflection:** Take time to reflect on your values, passions, and strengths. What truly matters to you? What activities bring you joy and fulfillment? What

unique gifts do you have to offer the world?

2. **Goal Setting:** Set clear and meaningful goals that align with your values and passions. Break down these goals into smaller, actionable steps that you can take each day to move closer to your vision.

3. **Taking Action:** Don't be afraid to take action and pursue your dreams, even if it means stepping outside your comfort zone or facing your fears.

4. **Building Supportive Relationships:** Surround yourself with people who support and encourage your growth and development. Seek out mentors, coaches, or peers who can offer guidance and inspiration.

5. **Embracing Challenges as Opportunities:** View challenges and setbacks as opportunities for learning and growth. Don't let fear or self-doubt hold you back from pursuing your dreams.

As you embark on this journey of self-discovery and personal growth, remember that thriving as an Enthusiast is not about achieving perfection or conforming to a certain mold. It's about embracing your unique gifts, navigating your challenges with grace, and creating a life that is authentic, joyful, and aligned with your deepest values and desires.

The world needs your enthusiasm, your creativity, and your unwavering belief in the power of possibility. By embracing your true self and living a life of joyful purpose, you can make a positive impact on the world and inspire others to do the same. So go forth, Enthusiast, and let your light shine!